INTIMATE EXCHANGES
Passion Paradies

INTIMATE EXCHANGES

Passion Paradies

Enjoying sizzling outbursts of exciting and nourishing poetry!

Nadine D. Clipper

ARPress
ILLUMINATING IDEAS.
EMPOWERING VOICES

ARPress
45 Dan Road Suite 5
Canton MA 02021

Hotline: 1(888) 821-0229
Fax: 1(508) 545-7580

Ordering Information:
Quantity sales. Special discounts are available on quantity purchases by corporations, associations, and others. For details, contact the publisher at the address above.

Printed in the United States of America.

| ISBN-13: | Softcover | 979-8-89330-388-9 |
| | eBook | 979-8-89330-389-6 |

Library of Congress Control Number: 2024903089

Table of Contents

Dedication Page...ix

Introduction xi

He Creates Clitorial Pudding!...1

From "Ho" 2 Wholesome! 2

Corn Field Fucking! 3

Jumping for Joy Kitty! 4

Get Ready Young Pony! 5

Open Letter: Dear Vagina! 6

All Night Room Service!...7

Stimulating Fingers! 8

You are Full of Wonders! 9

Please Share the Yum Yum Pie! 10

A Rewarding Embrace!...11

Glimpsing into the Future!...12

You Taste Like a Satisfying Sundae! 14

Feel the Fantasy! 15

Sexy Sunrise Surprise!...17

Love is in the Air for Sure! 18

Suck it or NOT, the Choice is Yours! 19

Attracting, Lip-Smacking, & Whacking!............................20

A Moment in Time! 21

A Sweet Fantastic Voyage! 22

My Sexy Caramel Drizzle!..23

Dripping with Intense Desire for Him! 24

Sexual Restoration!..25

Hey Sexy, It's Me!..26

Making Hypnotic Love in the Clouds! 28

The Aha Orgasm! 29

Simple Abundance! 30

Secret Love Affair to Share!...31

Your Private Dancer!..32

Wanna Be Your Candy Licker! 34

My Box is HOT for You!..35

Welcome! Thrilled You Joined the Fun......................36

It's Time to Show & Tell!..37

Going for a Sleigh Ride!...38

The Championship Trail!...39

Baby Come to Me!...40

Speaking in Positive Tongues! 41

Warm & Sticky Sensual Dessert! 42

Ding-a-ling, the Bell is Ringing!.............................43

Puss 'N Boots Rendezvous!....................................44

Naughty Holiday Cheers! 46

He's Knocking & Ringing the Bell!.........................47

Salute & Worship Fantasy Encounter 48

Sling Shooting Time!...49

Gobble! Gobble!..50

A Long Awaited Fortune! 51

HUGS...53

The Musical Horns Played a Blow Job Concerto! 54

Humpin' on the Hood!...56

Traveling Ventures! 57

Thank You! 58

A Lap Dance Tribute!..60

Lucky Charm! 61

Deep Desires to go Downtown!..............................62

Our Bodies Lie Over the Ocean...........................64

HOPE!...65

Sincerity 66

The Ding-A-Ling Swing! 67

Make It Do What It Do!..68

Please Me with Your Sexy Saxophone! 70

Encounters! 71

A Sexy Boy Toy!...72

Fuel the Friction with Mysterious Seduction! 73

Making Your Nature Rise!.......................................74

I Am Your Piece Lily!..75

The Venus Bag Surprises for You! 76

Craving a Caramel Delight! 77

Hey! Mr. Mocha Magic!..78

The Techno Love Routine! 79

I Desire You Inside Me! 80

My Horny Valentine! 82

Knock it out the Ballpark and Score!................................83

Lipstick on His Dipstick! 85

The Good Ship Lollipop!..86

A Powerful Make Out Session!...87

A Joyful Noise Mantra! 88

Welcome Spontaneity...Stimulating for Sure! 89

The Cum Back Kitty!...90

The Molecules Shift in Your Presence!..............................91

Refocusing on the Femininity Within! 92

Calling the Booty Bandit!...93

A Blackout Escapade of Pleasure! 94

Revolutionary Kitty Out-the-Box! 96

Ain't No Love like My Baby's Love! 97

Who's Loving Who? 98

Don't Tell the Truth...Don't You Dare! 99

When I Back it Up on You...! 100

Nutty Pleasures!..101

It's Quickie Time!..102

I Submit to Your "Billy Club" Fantasy Man! 103

Learning to Trust the Bondage Activity! 104

Flirtatious Devices!...106

Our Instant Connection! 107

Big Daddy CWI by Trade!..108

Sailing on a Sea of Fantasies!..109

Inconvenient Erotic Healing!..110

Silent Lover! 111

You Touched Me and Now...! 112

It's Just another Fun Day! 113

Mr. Water (H^2O) Bill Man!...114

Dedication Page

This anthology of poems is dedicated to all of you investing your time and resources to experience my art of poetry! To every person in the community in particular and those of you that will become honorary friends by supporting this project. Thank you for believing in this dream with me!

I am humble and grateful that you would share your time and mind with me on this seductive journey. It is my expectation that this collection of erotic poetry stimulate you enough to express your experience with others and that they will become excited too!

To my daughters for inspiring me to share my creative gift of poetry!

Introduction

The purpose of designing these poems is to ignite and stimulate the mind and fan the flames of ecstasy! This chronicle of poems was created to assist with ultimately bringing back unconditional love to relationships and encounters! These *Intimate Exchanges* poems are intended for adult viewers to obtain and share pleasure in mutually beneficial exchanges in real-time or fantasy. These creative lyrics are to generate stimulation that will keep the penis and vagina communicating in timeless sensational harmony that inspires infinite passion to experience multi-faceted orgasms!

First in the mind then all over the body! The arena of our mind is where the struggle begins and will end as long as we are aware of our inhibitions and commit to eliminating them. To win the battle between enjoying intimacy and just doing it, we must fuel our intellect with this collection of blissful tapestry lyrics! These succulent thoughts, imagination and desires are not based on any particular experience or person. To this end, I hope these quick-witted and intangible poems prepare your mind, stimulate your imagination, and make your body tremble to a point you will be dripping with . . . Let your imagination run wild and free with intense desires!

I am truly thankful to God for all gifts and talents that are bestowed on me and hope to utilize them to help create happier exchanges in the global community! I am optimistic that this collection of erotic exchanges will create and sustain natural cravings that continue to drive us wild infinitely!

Enjoy the journey of an abundance of great orgasms and revolutionary exchanges!

Relish in Excursions of Intimate Exchanges!

Nadine D. Clipper

He Creates Clitorial Pudding!

Creamy drippings streaming freely,
Like flowing rivers toward its destiny!
Stimulate the outing edges with your sweet fingers,
And make the sensation of your existence linger!

You make the kitty so wet with sweet extracts,
That only your thirst-quenching lips know how to attack!
You seem to enjoy exciting the kitty pudding,
As you play in it, stand erect and keep your footing!

No one tickles the clit like you,
Your touch is superior, and you know just what to do!
As you open the lips and stroke each side,
The dessert is ready as a result of your stride!

You make the best clitoral pudding in every case,
Keep doing your best stroking and you will win the race!
You see, not everyone can do what you do,
To make sure that the kitty is valued and true!

From "Ho" 2 Wholesome!

The clothes selection outlines her curves,
Most men lust to serve her swerve.
She is addicted to the attention,
From a man including those with false intentions.

She knows how to lure men,
Into her boobs to create new trends.
Then she moves on to the next one,
Because when she gets what she wants she's done.

Hos have and never will be loyal,
It is her role to temporarily make you feel royal!
Before you go there with her count the cost,
Before you get caught up in her rapture and are lost.

Then in the twinkling of an eye a manly man comes her way,
With his strength, loyalty, and purpose he makes her day!
As he loves her, she begins shifting from ho to wholesome,
Because all it takes is faith, courage, and wisdom to become one!

Corn Field Fucking!

What the hell is this all about,
This man wants to fuck in the fields without doubt!
Okay, how are we going to make this happen?
So that at the end of the session we will be dapping!

Show up at the fields in a dress and no panties,
Sharing this moment with him is a fantasy!
Go ahead drop all inhibitions and go for it,
Make that pussy sign for his dick!

You see, what you put in it is what you get,
The pleasure is in bending over and feeling his erect stick!
Wow, the amusement of fucking in the corn fields,
Makes the sexual exchange full of thrills!

When the chance to ride his juicy cock,
Takes you the fields, go with eagerness and make it rock!
The goal is to keep the sex life spunky and fresh,
Which allows nature to run its course and you will be impressed!

Jumping for Joy Kitty!

Kitty knows exactly what it likes,
Kisses, strokes, and lots of soft bites!
She loves to be caressed and tickled,
Then to skyrocketed by his luscious pickle!

Every time kitty sees him, she jumps for joy,
She gets juicy when she desires the toy!
Oh my, a blissful experience is anticipated,
The thrill of his dick is fun after kitty's been masturbated!

The delight of a celebrated kitty is bliss,
She shows her enthusiasm with hugs and kisses!
She grabs the dick with her succulent lips,
As she strokes the shaft and tip he is elated and ready for the trip!

A jumping for joy kitty is amazed with aroused pleasure,
She gets excited when he inspires her inner pleasures!
She will please the dick with her kitty tricks,
When she gets stimulated, she becomes wet and slick!

Get Ready Young Pony!

When older men date younger women,
Society sees this as okay and a sin.
Yet when older women date younger men,
It is played out like some new trend.

We love who we love, and it is what it is,
Girl, get your groove on and don't let the love fizz!
People need to get them some business of their own,
We don't need others' permission we are sexy and grown!

Women, get your young pony ready,
And ride him like a stallion gently rough and steady!
He likes it when you get on him and ride,
You are a winner in your pony's world so don't hide!

Show your energetic pony you got skills,
That will have him trembling with coolness and thrills!
Strive to make the experience a win-win for you and him,
You know you rocked his world when he treats you like a gem!

Open Letter: Dear Vagina!

Greetings Vagina! You are a precious commodity,
Created to serve with stimulation and harmony!
Oh honey, you are like a pearl in an oyster,
Your existence is bursting with heavenly moisture!

The way you do the things you do,
Everything falls to pieces in comparison to you!
Vagina, you make the world turn,
As you increase smiles and make everyone yearn!

Your lips become increasingly plumb and juicy to the touch,
With fingers, tongues and erect dicks make you want to fuck!
Your vagina monologue creates infinite sensations,
That causes man to make decisions without guided meditation!

Girl, you are the best creation since wine,
When you are loved and cared for you get better with time!
Giants have fallen because of your immeasurable impact,
This is no bullshit; I am just sharing the facts!

All Night Room Service!

You are all dressed up and ready for the date,
If the night goes as planned this maybe the mate!
The evening begins with a movie,
Do you like comedy, horror or pick one of these?

The movie was a great start,
The two of you were present and did your part!
Now it is time to decide on dinner, just remember keep it light,
Since it is going to take both of you all night!

There is a two for $20 deal at Applebee's,
This is a great option you will pleasurably agree!
The foreplay begins while seductively eating from the sample tray,
Eyes begin to glare; smiles increase and then bodies start to sway!

As hints about what will take place later are exchanged,
The sensations increase and you wonder is tonight going to be a boomerang!
You desire to be kissed, licked, and sucked,
As well as stimulated by getting long-stroked fucks!

After the first round then, it is up and down all night long,
Who knew that room service could bring a miraculous ding-dong!
Not to mention the kitty is providing dazzling profits as well,
Because every time you look around the dick swells!

Stimulating Fingers!

The anticipation of your needed embrace is too much,
Because it triggers stimulation and yearning for your touch!
When are you coming to satisfy this craving?
Come on and do what you do before the ranting and raving.

After all this time, your fingers still produces tingling to the spine,
As we start to get on you enter from behind…
Oh my, what excitement you're stirring up,
Then the experience turns silent with fingering and a freaky fuck!

Hold up, wait a minute the fingers are doing these tricks,
When reality sets in there was no action from your dick!
Your magical fingers are a wonder of creation,
That provides so much joy and surprising Sensation!

Stimulating fingers you are so wonderful for humanity,
As you gently remind us that you are more than a fantasy!
Thank you for keeping your skills up to date,
You are appreciated and needed without a debate!

You are Full of Wonders!

Yesterday you made a fantasy come true,
Today you said you were going to try something new!
This experience stunned the mind like never before,
Sparking ideas and total body vibrations Galore!

Where did you learn your creative skills?
They awaken the entire mind and body causing rare thrills!
The body was a sleeping giant waiting for you,
To satisfy its desires to cum once but you gave it two!

You are an amazement that never ceases with wonder,
The way you throttle, causing moans like thunder!
Keep slow rolling the kitty and make it have a heart-to-heart,
She speaks your language telling you to finish what you start!

You love what you do and are a hardworking man,
As well as making the kitty cum like only you can.
You are mighty with your long strokes and caressing cock,
You were created from some good seeds and celebrated stock!

Please Share the Yum Yum Pie!

As you sing sweet melodies in his tender ear,
He is sharing enchanting words soft and clear!
He triggers the sweat to trickle down your sensitive spine,
And provoke your skin to glisten, like sipping amazing wine!

Your bodies are rhythmically in sync,
Over to the left, up and down, he hits the hot spot then wink!
In the twinkling of an eye, he amazes you with a new move,
Catching you off guard, he rocks your body with his groove!

Shout it from the mountain to the valley what he did under your dress,
He made you a witness as you tremble and your soul confess.
His smooth performance says go run tell that?
After all he is the Big Daddy Mack!

Awwwww! Thanks for deciding to enjoy the dick work,
After you get a nut, he is ready to squirt.
Reach down and touch the balls with your tongue,
Yes, it is quite pleasing to hear him say a job well done!

A Rewarding Embrace!

The way you hugged me during our last dance,
Stirred something inside and now I'm in a trance!
Your unspoken love inspires me to remain still,
Even in the midst of our uncertainty, this thrill is real!

Hush Big Daddy not a mumbling word from you,
I feel you in my soul and this I know is true.
There will be times when I need a spoken word,
And yet in the quietness, your voice is still heard!

Keep dreaming of creative ways to capture our imagination,
I look forward to your rapture inspiring all of my sensations!
You did a great job surprising me with forbidden desires,
Thanks for pleasing my body, I am now inspired.

You deserve me dancing on your stick doing the wobble!
Get in there and watch me, Gobble!
I love you watching me sucking your BIG dick,
Then in a twinkling of an eye, I climb on it and sit with a split.

Glimpsing into the Future!

I project our love into the future because you are a keeper,
I learn from you each day as my life teacher!
Let's not forget our lessons in time, leader,
We are here to be each other's pleaser!

When it's time to invite me in your world freely,
We will build an oasis in solidarity!
You are all the man I need,
Let's make the time and plant love seeds!

You are so tasty just like fine wine,
Each episode gets better with time!
Thoughts of you tickle my spine,
Thanks for being wonderful and kind!

Yet, the temptation for a strong embrace,
Moves me to allow his love to shine in my face!
I am drenched in warm fuzzies for him,
I'm taking my chances and making a sex film!

You Taste Like a Satisfying Sundae!

You smell and taste like pure honey,
This makes sharing easy including the money!
When your flavor touches the tongue, sensuality is ignited,
Sparks of ecstasy tickles the kitty and she becomes delighted!

. . . .

You are the best dessert on the market,
And you are packaged like a rocket.
A little bit of this and a lot of that,
Triggers happy sensations so let's get on the mat!

. . . .

Your sundae textures get a lady to move,
Keeping her flexible that she doesn't need to find her groove…
The honeysuckle squirting from you is pampering,
What else do you have for the sampling?

. . . .

Store bought sundaes give unwanted calories,
But not your sweetness, it is healthy ecstasy!
Your beneficial pleasures are welcomed daily,
Awe! The satisfying after effect is a feeling of Glee!

. . . .

Feel the Fantasy!

Can we separate our sexual desires from our feelings without playing tricks?
Or do we crave sexual pleasure so much we lie on our pussy and dicks?
We say let me know when you want me to be what you need,
And I shall comply with bells and whistles to get your seed!!

As time passes, feel free to stay connected we say,
Because our friendship we cherish day by day!
Yet, we yearn to fulfill our favorite fantasy,
And we choose each other to express our inner freaky.

The pleasure is so intense we think the experience maybe long-term,
Until one of say this is just sex to release backed up sperm.
Yet, we play along believing decisions will be changed,
Then reality awakens us that our desires made us estranged.

Fantasies are healthy in the proper place,
Distinguishing facts from feelings keeps us out of space.
A puffed up penis is good but temporary,
Remind the pussy not to get fooled by sweet vocabulary!

Sexy Sunrise Surprise!

The aroma of your natural body scent,
Cleans the air through my nose vent!
As the early morning dew covers the grass,
Your hands are like gloves on my ass!

Your manliness shields me like a warm cover,
Soothing my need for a strong and special brother!
You are a sexy sunrise surprise,
And I am thankful that you are my prize!

Let's embrace each other with unrestricted adoration,
And nurture each other with spine tingling vibration!
As we witness each new day as it begins,
It is a thrill for us to be together when it ends!

I appreciate you and all your wonder,
Now it's time to share your sexy thunder!
Rock my body like you are suppose too,
And make my kitty rain like only you know how to do!

Love is in the Air for Sure!

I know my love is on the way, I can feel it in air,
This time it will be a tantalizing, freaky affair!
He will be all the man that I need,
So thrilled I waited to be pleased!

When we met, we thought we were uncertain,
Now we have history together and it's all pertinent!
Our talks, walks and connected affairs of ecstasy,
Has turned dreams into a reality!

Let's throw caution and limitations to the wind,
With bumping and grinding that makes us grin!
My body is craving to be all over you,
So make my kitty do what it is created to do!

When we have exhausted each other and it is all said and done,
We will be gasping for air like the championship has already been won!
Love is in the atmosphere within our reach,
Let's expand our desires as we learn and teach!

Suck it or NOT, the Choice is Yours!

Please don't say you will not,
Blow his cock on the spot!
If you are new to the sucking game,
Stick around and listen as I explain!

First, you must become one with the dick,
Enjoy it like a juicy Popsicle dripping from a stick!
The key is to make sure you are firm but gentle,
You can do it Girl, the success is mostly mental!

Second, the hands rhythm swag determines motions,
And will surely help the mouth's notion!
The moisture circulating in your mouth sets the tone,
So keep it clean and succulent to trigger his erogenous zone!

At last, he is moaning to the stroke of your appreciation,
As you wet and glide his dick with deep throat penetration.
Now, he is ready to share his vanilla toppings,
Decide ahead of time if you will swallow or decline before stopping!

Attracting, Lip-Smacking, & Whacking!

You see an enticing person; you want to know their name,
Before you approach, you think is this going to be real or just a game?
How can I hit that without a claim?
Will they play along or are they trying to be tamed?

So many of us in the single life treat love like a minor league thing,
We need to take risks by trying the true love swing!
Do a thorough self-assessment first and evaluate the results,
Then eliminate, anger, hate, distrust and abandon the insults.

Yes, we will have expectations of others and they will not deliver,
We will need to forgive them and set ourselves free even as we shiver!
When we invite love in, watch out, the attraction is contagious,
That we will recognize our light and we'll think it's outrageous!

This love game will bring many players to our gate,
It is up to us to enforce our standards and recognize the fakes.
Rise up and take a stand, there is someone who will mirror your desires,
And then make you weak in the knees eternally setting our souls on fire!

A Moment in Time!

There was a period of time when our love knew which way to go,
Then in a twinkling of a second it ended in sorrow.
What happen to trust, hope and sincerity?
Or maybe this experience was built on a mystery.

Our love had the appearance of positive energy,
We were in awe of one another and acted with generosity.
Our time together brought a lot of ecstasy and thrills,
That turned to heartache, tears and chills.

Where were the signs that could have protected me?
They were behind the feelings of bliss that I could not see.
Time has passed since we last met face to face,
It will be interesting to hear what all has taken place.

This sexual unveiling moment in time,
Is really perplexing to the body, spirit, and mind!
As the spirit creates an infinite thrilling heat,
The mind is convinced it desires a manly treat!

A Sweet Fantastic Voyage!

You know what I need and the intensity of our passion takes over,
As we slam and dunk dick and pussy lay ups under the covers.
Swoosh; swoosh; you hit the spot and make the shot every time,
These encounters demonstrate our best game and I'm overjoyed that you are
mine!

Write your name in my pussy with those enormous dick massages,
That makes me cry with joy that I crave you so much is this a mirage?
I just want to love you forever and dance on your dick,
Moving to your rhythm, do your thing Big Daddy, with your hard stick!

Yes, work your strong body between my hips,
And trigger my pussy muscles to grip it and introduce new tricks!
You do such a marvelous fuck job on me,
Then we exhale as we reach our peak of paradise in unity!

This event has cum to an end as we lay,
Embracing each other until the dawning of a new day!
As always, thanks for loving me and making sure I am satisfied,
I hope you are relaxed, thrilled to the core and mesmerized!

My Sexy Caramel Drizzle!

Your essence saturates my total being,
By awakening my multisensory system, am I dreaming?
Like the sun's reflection on the ocean,
you are a strong force with a peaceful commotion!

I crave your honey drizzling on me,
Warm to the touch and you taste so sweet!
Damn, this internal storm is creating sensitivity,
As the sweat pours down my body from your majesty!

Stand firm and penetrate me with your erection,
Oh la la! Can hardly wait for us to be sexing!
All these desires for you are escalating,
And they are so intense, I might start masturbating!

Thanks for the tantalizing drippings from your fountain,
Of sensuality as I climb you like a mountain!
I swerve my hips nice and slow,
As I dance your dick is so hard and full it's ready to blow!

Your sexiness ignites my taste palette,
I thirst to embrace your cocktail, can I have it?
I pledge to stroke it with my mouth just right,
Licking it as my favorite lollipop every night!

Dripping with Intense Desire for Him!

As the live jazz band plays,
Sensations whisper dance and let him feel my ways!
Is it the wrong time to give myself to you?
Are you ready for love that's tried and true?

What's come over my resistance?
I love the effect and it's persistent!
I surrender without old fears,
That if I allow him in, there will be few tears.

His rhythm is teasing my taste buds,
as I drip with desire for this stud!
His lips are kissable and inviting,
I accept his offer to be exciting!

He makes me feel special in his space,
As I stand my ground to win the Queen's place!
We will learn to love each other forever,
As a result, we will enjoy this endeavor!

Oh my! The intensity has me thinking with ecstasy,
Like a rose that radiates a prosperous journey!
Evolving into my true essence of a lady,
He intoxicates me with his alluring melody!

Sexual Restoration!

The awesome feeling of looking at a penis,
Ignites the sensation of the inner Venus!
Wow! The dick is a mighty wonder,
Hidden in a man's yearning to be discovered!

Swerve the curves of your hips,
It gets juicy as he licks his lips!
The teasing is triggering lust,
Will we take our time or get in a rush?

Yes, the stimulation is having an overwhelming impact,
But got to be sure the burglar doesn't get my Kit Kat!
I need help being restored,
Don't need to be played with like a toy!

Hold up, wait a minute, let's put something in it,
A set of standards to be clear if you are a fit!
This life is already peacefully unfolding daily,
What are you bringing to enhance my reality?

Hey Sexy. It's Me!

The relaxing Jazz and the illumination of the calming scented candles,
Ignites arousing thoughts of you getting it against the mantle!
I wish you were here to wrap your body around mine,
And allow our high temperature to warm us as we dance and whine!

I surrender to your tender touch that sets me on fire,
The way you heat my kitty is about to cause an explosion of desires!
Oh my, you kiss me ever so gently as you caress my mocha tits,
You make me moan with pleasure and I get a rise out of your joy stick.

Your arousing response salutes me very well,
Soldier, you are getting stronger as my tongue makes it swell!
Your stiff dick welcomes my wet tongue,
Baby, I know you like the way it feels and I am having fun!

You are a true fire starter and I am fascinated by the reality,
Of your fuck finger, prompting the thrilling juices to cum spontaneously!
The foreplay tickles my fancy and alerts me to get ready,
As you lay me down and lick my clit steadily.

I love your mouth tapping my spot until it responds with a tremble of ecstasy,
That produces this uproar of passion that is brewing inside my femininity.
The big show down positions us for the main event,
Yes, Big Daddy, this was a damn good fuck and like money I'm spent!

Making Hypnotic Love in the Clouds!

As the softness of the white cloud,
Tenderizes the mood, our moans get loud!
Our finger touching stimulates heat,
I wouldn't mind if your face is where I took a seat.

The shape of the clouds are carved with beauty,
Like our amazing connection is merging, spank my booty!
Provocative thoughts are sprinkled with your love,
Traveling through my being like a peaceful dove!

Gasping to regain control of my breath,
Your embrace makes me relax and take a rest!
Yes, your penetration is scary to me,
But peace is still as you and I become we!

Trust the Divinity in you to guide the journey,
Authentic love is our purpose and destiny!
Stop running soldier and stand your ground,
Taking an in-depth trip that's abound!

The clouds are fluffy and an oasis,
Just like our emotions can be tender with historical traces.
Extract the sensual flavors from the past,
They will allow us to build enchanting love that will last!

The Aha Orgasm!

You are transcending me Baby,
Helping me to be a fabulous lady!
I am evolving higher because I've met you,
And I am grateful that I can be myself too!

I am having a soulful awakening,
This experience is orgasmic and breathtaking!
The desires for you are so strong,
Is it possible for something so majestic to be wrong?

I am letting go of all fears and anxiety,
And granting myself permission to experience serendipity!
I release control and surrender all,
The future is bright and the past I will not recall.

I am imperfect with a hunger for excellence,
No more worries because standing with you I am magnificent!
Phobia is something I can release since you appeared,
It is only false evidence that makes me scared.

I am taking your advice and standing my ground,
Let's get busy loving and keep each other around!
Intuition tells me that your heart's desire is a reflection of mine,
The present moment is all we have; let's not waste another moment in time!

Simple Abundance!

You mentioned that your fingers are very sensitive on the top.
Are they delicate enough to tickle and make it hot?
The way you hold me and cuddle my booty, your fingers past the test,
Your touch is very penetrating I must confess.

I take you by the hand and seduce you under the stars after we dance,
When you boldly go under my dress and touch my clit it puts me in a trance!
To satisfy the cravings in the depths of my secrecy,
You have a wonderful way with your tongue that is juicy!

Just the thought of you loving me makes my spine shiver with ecstasy,
I get wet below as your tongue takes my body me on a fantasy!
As if your fingers and tongue didn't already get me caught up in the rhapsody,
you gently travel inside my luscious lips and work your magic in my kitty.

Oh my, the sensation has taken over me,
The amusement is intensifying and I am hot for your cock, Baby!
I am the luckiest girl alive because you make me satisfied,
It feels like "Disney World" I enjoy your adventure rides!

Thank you for kissing, holding and loving me like only you can,
You are a crafted specialist that's why I call you Big Papa, man!
I am thrilled beyond words every time I meet your big, strong cock,
Although the market is slow, I'm investing my money, you are good stock!

Secret Love Affair to Share!

It's been eight months since we met,
We laugh, love, chat and sweat!
Our connection is so powerful,
It reminds me of a government overthrow!

We meet weekly to keep the fire burning,
Sensual surprises are blazing inside and we are yearning!
The endless visions of our escapades, pleasures and thrill,
Keeps us caught up in the rapture because they seem real!

The world cannot understand how we think,
That makes it even more special because we are in sync!
Loving each other unconditionally is the mutual goal,
We cherish each experience because it's music for our soul!

When the time comes for us to depart,
We don't want to go and become distraught!
We hold on to each other like it's our last time,
Listening to our heart beats sounding like a wind chime!

Farewell my love until we meet again,
Remember out love craze is a win-win!
The day will come when our passion will be set free,
We will share it with the world just wait and see!

Your Private Dancer!

Stilettos, sexy lingerie, music for the soul,
It is show time I got to be bold!
I desire to outdo myself tonight,
I have this dance routine for him that's out of sight!

Moving my hips to the rhythm like a Señorita,
Dancing around the room like a cheetah!
Shaking my juicy booty, he grabs it with his hand,
The teasing and caressing is arousing my man!

I am introducing the portable pole in my recital,
Climbing and sliding up and down correctly is vital!
Wow! He is moaning and we are not on the sheets,
I love his reaction ~ he is in heat!

I continue to boogie for him to see,
Desiring to stroke him while inside of me!
As he captures and holds me, his touch is a mystery,
And I'm flexible enough to wrap my legs around his body!

The music fades and brings an end to the phase one act,
We are excited to a point of attack!
Stilettos keeping me balanced as I ride him like stallion,
Big Daddy is holding on to my hips he wins the medallion!

Wanna Be Your Candy Licker!

Licking on my neck, up and down my back,
Not yet, unwrapping the candy from the pack,
Unzipping his pants, his pecker jumps out of its trap!
Oh my, so sweet I'm having a panic attack!

It is delighted that I'm taking it for a ride,
Licking and stroking it on my tongue it glides!
His body moves with joy,
He feels the caressing of my wetness on his toy.

As I blow on the head of his cock,
The stimulation has him begging me to stop!
I keep licking him with passion as he likes,
Excitement is all over him like singing on a mic!

The tempo of my tongue ignites his moan,
Tickling him in surprising places all over him I roam!
Fondling the head, the balls, the prostate, the penis,
Amazing feelings are triggered within us!

Cuddling his candy in my mouth is firing me up,
His juices are watering my taste buds we may need a cup!
His lollipop is too big to finish in one setting,
Let's take a rest and then more sweating!

My Box is HOT for You!

Your smell is teasing every fiber of my being,
Inhaling your scent keeps the sensation lingering.
I'm stimulated by the movement of your hand,
Massaging and heating up my body, you are the man!

Your smile, I missed a good deal,
Your kisses make me shiver with a chill!
My hot box is boiling with desires,
Touching it, licking it, we are getting inspired!

Tell me what you want me to do,
I am here to serve you!
I love to stroke your bamboo stick,
I've been learning some sensual tricks!

When I get you behind closed doors,
You will get it on the bed, the shower, and the floors!
Kitty's been yearning for your magic touch,
Give her some attention like it's your lunch!

My box is hot,
Juices are steaming please tap my spot!
You turn on my kitty like a fountain,
Rocking your stick is like climbing a mountain!

Welcome! Thrilled You Joined the Fun...

You did your best work last night baby!
Thank you for the candlelit dinner and the wine was very tasty.
We need to make sure we keep it in stock...
Because it helped to reduce my anxiety and rock you around the clock.

I am amazed at how creative you were as our bodies met for the first time.
A night of passion and new ways of getting our freak on excited my spine.
You know what your woman needs,
and you are so wonderful to make sure I'm pleased.

It was a lot of fun when you blind-folded me and led me to a room,
...a trust exercise for sure it was like taking a trip to the moon!
As you undressed and escorted me into the bubbly jacuzzi,
The jets were pulsating against my body, I started feeling woozy!

Then in a twinkling of a second, it was on and popping,
The way you kissed me ignited the fire below...oh my, there's no stopping.
The heat is stimulating my kitty making it purr and call your name,
Your fingers have rights of passage into my bliss you get the credit and blame!

As you massaged the inner and outer kitty lips,
I open up and allow you to have your way as you nibble and sip.
Get it Big Daddy, make it drizzle and exclaim with glee,
Thanks for heeding the call, the sensation was so intense, I took a plea!

It's Time to Show & Tell!

Last year was a time to experiment with the mysterious,
We tried different things because we were curious.
Now that a year has come and gone,
We are challenged to stay or do we move on?

❤ ❤ ❤ ❤ ❤ ❤ ❤ ❤

I pledged in the beginning that I was in it to win it,
Your heart is what I'm after and I will not quit.
So, act like you don't care if you want to,
This experience is making a better me and you!

❤ ❤ ❤ ❤ ❤ ❤ ❤ ❤

As you often remind me timing is everything,
I encourage you to remember, we are humans not machines.
Love comes and changes our plans,
We need to remain focus while we dance!

❤ ❤ ❤ ❤ ❤ ❤ ❤ ❤

Hold me in your arms and rock with me,
Wow! As you arouse my sexual organs, I am horny!
Your nature rises as you move to the beat,
Let's get in the Expedition and share our treat!

❤ ❤ ❤ ❤ ❤ ❤ ❤ ❤

You are a heaven on earth type of man,
After our lovemaking we travel to Dreamland!
As we hold each other so strong,
I hear your voice singing our favorite song!

Going for a Sleigh Ride!

After a long day of work,
want to get home and flirt?
We have date night to decide,
And I desire a sleigh ride.

The bed is going to be dessert for us,
The thrills from all the foreplay intensifies our lust.
as we dine and dance most of the night,
Dripping with hot, sweaty delight!

The clock tells us get to the dessert,
Oh my, the goal is to make our juices squirt!
We begin at cruise control speed,
and then plateau as he takes the lead.

He is like Santa leading the reindeers,
As our bodies tremble with cheers!
The air is misty with our sensual smell,
Shhh, the freaky things we are doing, we can't kiss and tell!

Tis the season of giving our sleigh ride was a success,
We are back from paradise and need a rest!
Thank you Big Daddy for the ride,
Jolly as can be, we smile at each other with pride!

The Championship Trail!

He takes me by the hand on a trail of rose pettles leading to his bed,
As he removes the blind-fold, I surrender by giving him head.
Before I let his bamboo stick sprout its juice,
I engulf as much as my mouth can handle before I turn it loose!

You have such a huge cock, I have to take it easy or get chocked,
The vapor of my tongue gliding up and down your cock, you enjoy the stroke!
The way you sway your hips indicates the highest point of your hard on,
Oooh, the time has come for us to dance like its done in the porns.

In the midst of getting ready for our show down you surprise me,
by getting a taste of kitty, it feels like I'm climbing a tree.
You hit the spot and I quivers like never before,
What are you doing to me, I whisper gently as we do it on the floor?

What does it feel like you reply?
As your dick travels inside my island its so good, I begin to cry.
All the thunder and lightning created while satisfying our urge,
The way you nurture me is astonishing as our bodies merge.

We did in the bed, on the floor, the kitchen counter, and there's still more,
Wow! how amazing and mind blowing our connection as you pin me to the door!
It's like we're competing for the global championship and both of us want to win,
As we fade from the intense workout, breathing rhythmically we set a trend!

Baby Come to Me!

It's been a long time since we've gotten together,
Time and space is great do we still choose each other?
I yearn to smell your satisfying scent,
Hold me close in your arms to create quality time spent!

How will we spend our precious time on Sunday?
A picnic in the part, walk and talk, how long can you stay?
It's been months since we made love under the star lights,
Stimulating each other, triggering our sensual delights!

So bring your honey dew self to me,
I am dripping with all kinds of surprises you will see.
You are in my thoughts, body and soul,
Sometimes your presences is so strong, it takes control.

Thoughts of you make me hot and crave you sexually,
Reminiscing about past encounters trembles my body!
You see, your love making has a lasting impact,
Not trying to swell your ego, only stating true facts!

Get ready for an exciting experience between the two of us,
We'll begin slow and then elevate our lovemaking to robust!
Big Daddy! I am going to tickle you caringly,
I have been yearning for you because our time together is a commodity!

Speaking in Positive Tongues!

One day when I was walking down the street,
A fine man turned around and said he picks me.
Pick me to do what, I responded with a smile?
He said to be my lady for a while!

I said, no thanks I am a keeper,
He said give me a chance to make you a believer.
Awhile is temporary and I am infinity,
He mentioned that our meeting is serendipity!

I thought for a moment that he could be my soul mate,
What if I give him a chance to prove himself, wait what's at stake?
It takes a long time to recover from a heart break,
Not if I trust in love and step out on faith!

He was speaking in tongues initially,
Now, I understand his language as we blended our energy..
He asked me to be his companion for life,
I'm hesitant because I love peace and don't do strife.

He assures me there are no guarantees on life's journey,
I know this intellectually just not sure emotionally.
Take a risk on me and you will see,
I will love your mind, body, and soul unconditionally.

Warm & Sticky Sensual Dessert!

Warm, mouth-watering sweetness,
Teasing our taste buds with greetings!
Awakening sensations are triggering desires,
Intoxicating our essence making us perspire!

Our connection is motivating fun,
Keeping us excited as the rising sun!
Our beauty is illuminating amazing sensuality,
the time is now with an abundant mentality!

We are feeling the sticky chemistry,
That has us yearning each other as a fantasy.
Do we try and stop holding out,
Or do we hesitate and live with doubt?

I'll stand in your presence without taking charge,
You are the leader and this not a mirage!
Trust the process and embrace the fascination,
As you Sprinkle me with your warm & sticky temptation!

Then in the nick of time,
Uncontrollable sensations tickle our spine!
Please plan to take me on a life time trip,
As we make love our passionate juices drip!

Ding-a-ling, the Bell is Ringing!

As we awaken to alarm bells ringing in our ears,
Viola! my hands wonder under the cover and grab his spear!
His hard ding-dong is screaming I need you to release me,
Those morning stiffs are a great day starter, begging to be free!

As I sneak under the covers and gently warm up the prize,
With tongue strokes, it swell like hives.
Yeah, baby suck that pipe just like that he states,
So, I continue saluting him with my mouth until he's ready to mate.

No need to waste a hard on as I climb and give it all I had!
He said "get it please baby please…" thanks for the invite that makes me glad!
This wonderful man of mine is always ready to begin our day,
With lots of thumbing and a steamy session of foreplay!

Juices are flowing and swooshing as he inserts that magic finger once more.
OMG…was he dreaming about what to do this morning to make me sore?
I already produced two orgasms and he has yet to inject me with the Dick,
That I cherish so much as he penetrates, I'll show him a trick.

Our bodies are in sync as we are roll around, pulling sheets off the bed,
Because the excitement takes over as he go deep inside to awaken what's dead!
As he swivels to the left and I go to the right the passion intensifies,
The pace increases then we slow down and hurry up again, making sure we satisfy.
Ding-a-ling, we answer when we hear the bell ring!

Puss 'N Boots Rendezvous!

We met for dinner and drinks at a Hotel Bar,
Girl, this man is so sexy what a star!
My hormones are alerting me to paste a kiss on his smiling lips,
He willingly cuddled me with his manly hands on my hips!

I was weakened by his touch for what seemed like eternity,
He better watch out because I am feeling really frisky!
Tonight we will do some role playing,
Since we have all night at the hotel we are staying!

I was Odyssey the queen and he was the mighty king Zeus,
Inhibitions were left at the door and our goal was to be wild and loose!
We are being quite risqué and yet so willing to give new delights,
The kissing and touching began and continued throughout the night.

Our hands travel all over our bodies and before long clothes are flying to the floor,
He lifts me onto the table and began licking me up and down and there's more!
Not to be out done, I give him a special beat down with oral stimulation,
As I take charge and caress his bat and balls with sensation!

As we surrender to the enthusiasm we have for each other,
Drips of sweat tiptoe down our bodies and hotness rises on the covers!
He starts knocking my boots with throbbing penetration,
The potency of our yearning appetites continues with fascination!

Naughty Holiday Cheers!

May each day bring you the naughtiness you desire,
A lot of Dancing, Prancing and Romancing, get inspired!
Keep a merry heart, full of festival cheer,
Sensual singing, swinging, and plenty of beer!

Dashing and flashing in Santa's helper attire,
Fa, la, la, la Big Daddy you set me on fire!
Presents to wrap, parties to attend oh my, the time is here,
As we head out the door, he stops me and wants if from the rear!

Time is passing faster than ever,
We have to go as we breathe heavier!
I feel your sling shot cumming, let it go in my planter,
Wow! Cheers to you my sexy Santa!

Back to the shower and out the door we try once more,
I be damn, hot and horny we are fucking on the floor!
The parties will be over and we didn't get to attend,
We adore each other's bodies it's been like traveling!

During the Christmas, Kwanzaa, and holiday seasons,
Be reminded you are cared about you for so many reasons!
We've spanked each other with TLC really good,
Naughty thoughts, turned into action that we both understood!

We'll drink to that…Cheers!

He's Knocking & Ringing the Bell!

After he's been working hard all day,
I am doing all I can to arrange my schedule for us to play!
As his confidant, I need to be available to ensure that he gets what he requires,
Because eventually he will be mine full-time and I have to handle all desires.

It is all about the recruiting and retaining process,
Shhh! he is the #1 draft pick I must confess!
Yes, I am courting him to sign with my franchise.
Once he gets out of his current contract, he will start on my team just in time.

We are in negotiations and I am going to delight him like no other,
With that being said, I have established winning guidelines for this brother!
He is going to be filled with glee when I am done rocking his world,
I have been waiting to dazzle him with my sexy twirl!

At last he is ringing the bell and knocking on the door,
I was expecting him later than he arrived; I'm trembling at the core.
He is here now so excuse me while I welcome my man,
So glad he could join me and I take him by the hand!

We have small talk and then ended with peeling off clothes, kissing and touching,
Inhaling and exhaling each other's breathing pattern while sucking!
We have this chemistry that explodes when we are together!
Our bodies are connected and that makes our escapades last forever!

Salute & Worship Fantasy Encounter

It is indeed an honor and privilege to share with you daily,
I worship you for being such a wonderful man and treating me fairly!
As I anticipate your every touch, my skin tingles with delight,
And I get really excited because you make sure that I am alright!

You are my vibrant toy...full of life and fairytale pleasures,
You don't need batteries to satisfy me, your stiff dick is a treasure!
You are my paradise and I take a trip to heaven on earth every time you fuck
me!
My kitty leaps for you automatically is this a fantasy?

You gently rock my booty and we move to the rhythm,
Especially Lil Wayne's How to Love this tune is a gem!!
Thank you for enhancing my imagination, since I met you,
I dream of ways to satisfy every sexual desire and make it come true!

Tell me how you want it...in lingerie, naked, wrapped in a bow or a thong?
Because your wish is my command and I will work hard all day long!
Your kisses increases my heart rate,
And a sexual rush of desire, takes over making me ready to mate!

Sling Shooting Time!

Thank you for taking care of me every week,
You are in a class by yourself like a championship sweep!
It is a pleasure to know that our "Date Night" excites you like it does,
In the words of Sam Cooke, You Send Me...Honest You Do and you say it's
because!

You always make sure that I have enough to drink,
And you dance with me like we are the only ones in the room, I love this link.
We are building a solid foundation that includes all that we desire and need,
You have this amazing sensual nature that fascinates me with deeds!

I crave your touch, smell, voice, and piercing eyes undressing me with
authority,
It's sling shooting time; let's make plans to ensure our mission is a reality!
Getty up my rodeo king…make my booty go boom, boom, boom,
I love the way you grab my ass and make it shake to your own tune.

As you prepare to release the sling, we get sidetracked since we are just
warming up,
Our destination is still miles away, so hold our fire below and not let it erupt.
It is wet with anticipation of us fucking like swiftly thrown rocks
That is rippling in the sea of passion as so noted by your hard cock!

At last, we are at our destination to partake of the island's party,
it's time to hit the target with your firm sling shooter don't be tardy!
Wow! The mission is complete, because the target has been hit,
And the juices are flowing from being struck with that big dick.

Gobble! Gobble!

Now that Thanksgiving Day has come and gone,
We need to take a walk by the pond.
Family and friends are out of the way,
I am thankful it's just for a day!

It is so sexy to imagine our time together,
Our fingers are tightly interlocked forever.
Did you eat enough of everything?
I ate turkey necks, thinking it was your ding-a-ling.

Questions were asked as I enjoyed sucking you,
I'm practicing my slurping skills to be tried and true!
Extracting your juices is appetizing,
The feeling I am going to give you will be tantalizing!

You are "tapping out" and begging me to quit!
But you told me if I go there you can handle my tricks!
I gently insert your entire long dick!
Can't choke me, I know when to go deep and when to lick!

I am dancing on your stick doing the wobble!
Get in there and watch me, Gobble! Gobble!
I love when you watch me grind your dick,
Show me how to love you as I climb on it and sit.

A Long Awaited Fortune!

This is a note to let you know that I miss you so much!
Thought our dancing was stimulating like a sock it to me punch!
What's been up, why haven't you kept in touch?
Is it possible for us to schedule a rendezvous lunch?

I will wait as long as I can for your return.
Please come back to us with lessons learned.
Separation is a good thing to develop potent sperm.
Shoot me with your big, juicy worm.

Your love stimulates my clit.
Causing my thighs to open into a split!
Cum get it King; take your tongue and lick, lick!
Damn, you're good I feel you slinging your super-size dick!

You and I are destined to be!
Our time apart is to prepare us for eternity!
Life is shaping us for our unity!
Are you ready for infinite prosperity!

Trusting you to do what you said you will do!
All I have is your word, is it true?
Or are you just a talking head, causing me to be blue?
Is this an experience you still want to pursue?

HUGS

I hope by the time your heart is penetrated with thoughts of me,
Your soul cries out with glee!
It's been a few weeks since we laid eyes and hands on each other.
I hope all is well and that you haven't gone and found another!

Is it because you are working on your two-year plan you shared intensely?
Since I am unsure, I give you time and space without acting defensively.
I feel sad sometimes because I am not sure where I stand with you.
I stopped communication because my heart says for me to.

We have to live our lives to the fullest and prepare for each other with diligence,
If this goal is mutual we need to work out the details and commit with persistence!
I am thrilled to spend quality time learning what you need,
As I discover my role with you planting seeds.

Seeking truth and clarity regarding why we are in each other's lives,
Knowing that all things happen for us to strive.
As I dream really BIG I invite you to dream BIG also.
Come out of your comfort zone and be amazed at how you glow!

The Musical Horns Played a Blow Job Concerto!

As the horns play, it's time to perform the blow job mission,
The horns are woodwind instruments as the dick is man's composition.
The initial tune plays from the flute on the hill in the truck,
The sounds are fabulous as the mouthpiece surrenders to a great fuck!

As a hard worker a man needs some head to get through his process,
A blow job clears the mind like realizing your true quest.
Is this really happening or is it a fantasy?
It's real and she loves blowing his saxophone to relax his body.

Wow, she is a miracle performer,
As she satisfies his cravings the melodies say keep her!
She is one in a million and a keeper in his band,
Her talents extend to the harmonica and the moans are from her hand.

It's the beginning of the week and his dick is being ignited like dynamite,
Her lips are closed as she blows her hardest just right!
All the notes harmonize effortlessly as she blows him superbly!
The erection of his pipe tells the story of her sold out symphony.
Applause! Applause!

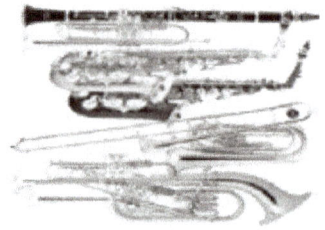

Humpin' on the Hood!

Today is the day for us to hump on the hood of your car!
So slide your shaft in my vulva and get the engine ready because you are a
star!
I have pulled up to your bumper baby and ready to travel with you!
Can you focus on this steaming pussy and drive too?

Check my vitals because my radiator is about to overheat with desire of you
sexing me.
I need you to bump and grind with your long hose cooling off the hot spot you
can't see.
You are the only mechanic, who can utilize his dip stick,
To check under my hood with your stiff dick.

As you look under the hood of my red fishnet and gently respond, "Can't slow
down,
I am on the highway of passion and your radiator is singing a hot sound.
I got to keep rubbing this kitty with my dick until your fluids are drained.
Wow! The way you power steer that cock in my pussy make my juices rain.

Now, we have alternated our position and you lay me on my stomach while
driving,
that stiff dick in through the rear axle... not there, keep striving!
Ooh lah lah! That move hits the spot and makes the engine run,
It seems everything is working and we pass the inspection of erotic fun!

Just when I think you are done, you squeeze my taillight and inform me that
all is okay,
Thank you Mr. Mechanic for checking my vitals, nothing more to say!
You are the world's best mechanic with your talents and skills,
Your ability to remember and recall key information keeps me thrilled!

Traveling Ventures!

I hope you are having a great day,
Please note that I am consumed with stimulating thoughts of you in a sweet
way!
Thoughts of the night the stars will watch us embrace each other's deepest
need,
Your touch warms my soul, your smell excites and lingers with slow speed!

No, silence isn't so bad as long as we can dialogue and connect,
To share thoughts that are not always convenient or comfortable to detect!
I do not argue and I do not have to be right.
The truth speaks for itself and I do not have to prove a point to have insight.

You are so wonderful and I am excited that we met that special instant,
A new opportunity presented itself for us to be transparent!
I have shared some of my deepest most intimate thoughts,
Because I am assaulting some assumptions I've been taught!

I am hesitating to share much more because of where you are on your journey,
I don't want to cause you turmoil as you strive to reach your destiny!
You deserve to be happy and to have a peaceful life!
You have been unhappy and unloved far too long dealing with strife!

Thank You!

Thank you for helping to make my dreams come true,
Heaven must be missing an angel because I now have you!
It is amazing that someone with your swag is interested in me and not the rest,
Yes, I deserve the best and here you are putting my belief to the test!

Thank you for demonstrating that love is a sure thing,
Now tonight, it is with pleasure that I sex you like having a secret fling.
This pole dance session is to show you how much I appreciate you in my life,
So, sit back, relax, and enjoy the saturating melodies once and surprisingly
twice.

My favorite song is playing and I begin to swivel around teasing the pole,
I become one with this exotic stick because my man needs to be assured of my role!
This is a lot of fun as I wrap my leg around the pole and glide up and down,
He is so amazed that he doesn't make a sound!

Oh my! This is a thrill to be able to perform this amusing activity,
To let this gentleman know how much I appreciate his sensuality.
I am blossoming into this spontaneous woman and he deserves the praise,
Because he encourages me to be my best self and I continue to be amazed!

I fight the urge to undress him as the foreplay heats things up,
Our touching and tasting senses are activated; nectars are boiling and about to
erupt!
His cock has pitched a tent in his pants and he cannot suffer any longer,
I unzip them to thank him and give his dick room to get stronger.

A Lap Dance Tribute!

Here is your exclusive VIP invitation for a private dance,
Baby, I desire to dazzle you with honeydew romance!
We are all alone in the candlelit bedroom,
With enticing aromas as eagerness looms!

The seductive voice of Ron Isley, provokes the dancer in me,
As I drop my robe and reveal the lingerie for your eyes to see!
Are you ready to nibble on my chocolate morsel Tits? They are semi-sweet,
As you watch with a smile, I bounce them like a holiday treat!

I desire this tribute to arouse your greatness as the night begins,
Awakening your taste palette and provoke the hardness in your pants again
and again!
The melody from the background music urges me to rotate my hips,
Like a figure eight (8) that motivates you to join me on this sensual trip.

As you squeeze my ass gently yet intensely, I continue dancing while you
watch,
And you remain stirred up because you put my hand on your crotch.
Baby, Thank you for not rushing the end because we have lots of time to do it
right,
Oh yes! with erect nipples and loose hips I invite you to participate in a
thrilling night!

We are enthralled in a moment of passion and heavy-duty stimulation,
Our hands are all over one another in pure unified sensation!
Oh my! The penetration of your fingers alert me to the reality,
That it's time to fuck you vigorously and help set you free!

Lucky Charm!

We couldn't wake up next to each other on this rainy day,
Nonetheless, make it the best ever without delay!
Go get them tiger…do your thang and make it fall in place,
I am proud of you for winning life's cheerless race!

Baby, while you are working, know that I need you all over my body,
I love the way you send chills up my spine as you put your thang on me!
I feel you tapping your dick on my booty, it feels splendid,
Thank you for taking me along for the ride our chemistry is blended.

Allow me to tease your dick with my fingers until you say let's go,
To the side as I squat and take a lick until you grow!
The pulse of your heartbeat is beating in your cock,
Oh my! What a sensation it makes me want to moan and bark!

You make the clit's forecast drip with scattered showers,
What a thrill, you give and you say it gets better by the hours?
As we continue touching and feeling; kissing and yearning,
Our eyes and bodies are filled with blissful burning.

Your stamina causes kitty to trickle cum all over you… Ahhh! what a relief,
Thank you sweetie, for protecting me as my chief!
Now that our minds are clearer and we are focused and geared up,
Are you pleased Lucky Charm with this spontaneous fuck?

Deep Desires to go Downtown!

Jockeying the kitty like it's a horse,
Hiding in the exciting moment with penetrating force!
A tickling sensation excites the spine,
While he's licking up & down from behind.
Dipping in the secret erotic zones,
Seeking ecstasy in places of stone.
As we anticipate the outcome of each amazing round,
The trembles will be like taking a field trip downtown!
Fabulous delights are stirring up many thrills,
As his touch activates breathtaking chills!
The wetness of his kiss,
Opens the legs of her bliss.
Exploring avenues that have not been completed,
His tongue strokes seem like a serene retreat just got heated.
The lip lashing is a fantasy come true,
He is incredible when he makes it do what it do!
He gives direction to the shooting juices,
As it flows out like a fire hydrate's water use!
Dripping with refreshing appetites,
To explore new arousing passions and get it right!

Our Bodies Lie Over the Ocean...

Yes! At last we made it to our vacation get-away.
Our souls are soothed by the scenic beauty each day!
We will need nourishment after plenty of sexual play,
Because there will be little outside activities, I must say!

As the oceanfront view pierce our hearts and generate peace,
Sharing this beautiful time with someone special, all worries cease!
We cuddle the blue skies with our eyes and inhale the fresh ocean smell.
Our senses are ignited, as we embrace each other because all is well.

The sensation from our contact creates ecstasy,
That's been a long awaited fantasy!
Our connected hands are moistened by the sexual tension that is building.
The playful brush against his erected crotch intensifies the tingle that is
yielding.

He really excites me and it is more than I can stand,
As he grabs me by the waist ever so gently, he is a strong man!
While passionately kissing, he elevates his hands up my dress,
And I respond by unzipping his pants and caressing his stiff, can't tell the rest!

Our breathing volume increases, and the clothes are rearranged by our
roaming hands,
We are over stimulated with thrilling moans and erected commands!
The heightened intensity brings us to our peak performance,
As we glide back and forth, up and down, changing positions takes a lot of
endurance!

HOPE!

Your presence is strong in me for some reason,
I feel your hands on my body, is it mating season?
Also, a tingle in my kitty sent visions of your rocket,
Traveling around my solar system exciting my socket!

I will wear something special under my dress for your eyes,
So check at your leisure I guarantee you there will always be a surprise!
Wishing we can have time alone after our dancing,
We need to go to our special place under the stars for romancing!

I need to taste your big dick throbbing in my moist mouth,
Pleasing my palette, satisfying my hunger then go down south!
I am thrilled by how you make my kitty juices crave your injection,
Please baby, please unclog my pipes with electrifying sensation!

As the melodies play softly in the background,
My fantasy of you is over as my hormones settle down!
Dreams are lived twice, first in the mind then in reality!
I know we will meet soon because I believe in the work of the Almighty!

I truly miss and yearn for you something crazy,
As I strive to take my mind off you in this moment is amazing!
I'm feeling for you and it's hard to refocus,
Are coming over to be my main course?

Sincerity

I woke up this morning with desires of you tickling my spine,
I am proud and inspired by you at the same time!
A sensual visual of you caressing my body,
Was all over me and I returned the gestures harmoniously.

As I was squeezing your nipples and rubbing your chest,
Your excitement informed my hands to travel and explore the rest!
I began stroking that long, strong bat as though I was hitting a home run,
Then I switched it up to keep it interesting and you were stunned!

My hot, juicy mouth wanted to be in on the action,
Let's not forget those succulent balls calling for a lip-lashing!
I started licking and gently cuddling those precious jewels,
Oh my goodness was your response as I use my tongue tools!

It's moaning time as I rhythmically entertain your pulsating dick aching,
To enter my kitty and unclog my faucet with some lovemaking!
Okay, slide inside my wetness and rock my internal flame,
Until it erupts with ecstasy as I will never be the same!

Ahhh! At last, you work your magician tongue on my clit,
And let it know that you are the man to take me on a trip.
What a relief it is for us to reach our peak as one,
Heavy breathing and smiles fill the room because our best work was done!

The Ding-A-Ling Swing!

Wow! What a big dick you possess,
I want to ride it out for a test!
Awww, it feels mighty good inside,
My wet kitty makes it slip & slide.

You have great stamina with your style.
As we groove for many miles.
The sweat is dripping from your body to mine,
You are truly working me out as you jiggle my behind.

We can't get caught up in this magical swing,
Until we determine if this is real attraction or just a fling?
You know you want me for more than a "booty" call,
I'm available to catch you so let yourself fall!

I will drive near and far,
To dance with you my twinkling star!
Let's not do the cat and mouse play,
We can agree it's going to be different today!

What do you really desire from a lady?
I can do those things and not go crazy!
Let your imagination come alive,
As we enjoy each other because your sex has a seductive drive!

Make It Do What It Do!

As we meet and greet,
our charisma generates intense heat.
Are we going to do the damn thing as a yearning?
Or strive to stay long term and keep learning?

We are bringing our best to the game,
making our bodies do what they do without shame!
Wow! Your body is strong and tight,
I desire to make you my mocha delight.

Hold me close to your heart,
Remember to finish what you start!
Today is a great day for us to do it again;
We are very excited so where do we begin?

Kiss me gently and tickle my spot,
As I wet your whistle and get you hot.
We will get better with time,
By learning how to love and be kind!

Thanks for being compassionate and strong,
Guess what, I'm wearing a red thong.
As the sun turns to the moon,
I hope we have another encounter soon!

Please Me with Your Sexy Saxophone!

May the melody of my thoughts penetrate your heart,
Remember that practice makes perfect before you start!
I am listening and hugging every word you say,
Big Daddy, your rhythmic sounds makes it a great day!

The touches of your sensitive fingers tickle my spot,
Holding me close on the dance floor causes my booty to pop!
Take your hand and perform under the stars,
For a night of ecstasy as you stroke me with your bars!

During this encounter, boldly insert your fingers and play your best,
The invention of these tunes creates stimulation I must confess!
Your sexiness puts a Kool-Aid smile on my face,
In a matter of minutes, my juices will be flowing in this place!

As if your touches weren't enough to satisfy my musical desire,
Your tongue reaches the depths of my secrecy and makes me perspire!
Will you do that thing you do with your lips?
Oh my! Those sounds send my body on a passionate trip!

The way you grab your saxophone amuses my spine,
You truly have mastered your gift for all time!
I get wet below as I blow your horn,
Feeling your greatness a new sound is born!

Encounters!

Oh my, a sensation has taken over me…
I am the luckiest girl alive because I have a man that won't flee!
It takes courage to run a marathon with his tongue,
Through my river of ecstasy we have just begun!

The stimulation is intensifying and I am hot for your cock!
As I drown in desire you have increased your stock!
As you dip fingers and tongue in my rapture,
And gently find your way inside my lusciousness, I'm captured!

You are magical with the way you work my kitty,
I am thrilled beyond words every time you suck these titties!
It is a delight to meet your big, strong bamboo stick,
It seem like I went to "Hollywood" to star in a flick!

Keep performing like you are playing for a championship,
The way you score points prepared you for the trip!
When you exit my playground, I will act like you cast a spell!
Thank you for the adventure, I will show more then I tell!

Until we meet again, on the dance floor, under the stars and moon,
Thank you for kissing, holding, loving me and I hope to see you soon!
Our connection is so awesome that I am rendered speechless,
Thank you for teaching me how to embrace my uniqueness!

A Sexy Boy Toy!

Young and gifted with a flavorful hue,
Honeydew dripping from his lips, he's says I want you!
I'm digging what I see,
And you need to be with me!

Boy please, I'm an older woman what do you need?
Do you just want to play with me No he pleads?
I am a franchise team owner,
I'm recruiting for a starter player that's not a loner.

Play with heart in every game,
Swooshing your shots as you strive to maintain!
Palm my booty with your manly hands,
Stunning me with freakiness as you take a stand!

You may be young but you're ready,
Entertaining and giving it to me steady.
Yes I'm older with staying power,
Putting kitty on you and making it produce rain showers!

It is thrilling to nurture my toy,
Giving and receiving brings tremendous joy!
He's sexy and strong in his independence,
He has seductive skills and a conversation that makes Sense!

Fuel the Friction with Mysterious Seduction!

My total being comes alive when you are near,
Vibrating like a melodic sound in your ear!
Ooh Baby! You take my breath away,
Did I win the lottery or is it payday?

Your swag is just as unique as your DNA,
As you move with your manly sway!
Touch and Draw me close to you,
As you rock me tenderly and make me your Boo!

Set me on fire with your arousing energy,
As we relax and sip on Hennessey.
Our sensual desires are heating up fast,
As we stimulate each other, he touches my ass.

We develop comfort as we explore and tease,
Touching, tasting, and then we please.
Awww, the sensation is mouth-watering and strong,
As I stroke his dick, he rips off my thong!

We use a captivating approach to take care of our needs,
Our bodies shake in harmony and we are well pleased.
We gently kiss and touch as we bring this session to a close,
When he returns to the room he presents me with a precious rose!

Making Your Nature Rise!

When our sexiness met, we both felt the vibe,
We want each other as our attraction comes alive!
Every time you see me coming, I make your nature rise,
Just when you think you know, I mystify you with a surprise!!

The fascination we have is urging us to try,
And size each other up or keep moving and say goodbye.
Our voices begin to arouse our being,
As the charm demands us to start pleasing,

Hold up wait a minute we just met,
If I give into you too early you will jet.
Please don't forget you asked me to be your girl,
Let's do it together and be the best in the world!

I will keep you satisfied and thrilled,
Every experience will be like a boot camp drill!
You can burglarize my kitty on a regular base,
Sending tingles up and down our spine with our strong embrace!

The raw and powerful stimulation causes trembles,
Sending sparks flying like playing musical symbols.
The smooth sounds create instant release,
As this journey ends we land in abundant peace!

I Am Your Piece Lily!

We are hippity, hopping on the happy trail.
Opening ourselves like a flying kite, we set sail!
Swim in my kitty while palming my butt;
Work it out baby until you bust a nut!

You taste sweet like chocolate chip morsels,
Gliding up and down to the shape of my torso!
My lips are blossoming like a flower,
Quenching my thirst for your penetration in the shower!

I am thrilled how you stimulate and get me all wet,
and deliver peak performance as we quiver and sweat!
It is amazing how limber and flexible your body plays with me,
As you get better with time keep giving with endless glee!

Your classy level of risqué thoughts and deeds,
Ignites my juices to flow with uncontrollable speed!
I appreciate your magical lovemaking skills,
They mesmerize my mind and body with treats and thrills!

Keep the wonder alive through the test of time,
I will do whatever you need to keep you mine!
No other can make the music we create as one,
After each love dance, our get-up-and-go is done!

The Venus Bag Surprises for You!

Fishnet panty hose, vibrators and lingerie,
The Venus bag must be ready for a sensual soirée!
Let's not forget the sex games and hints of fairy dust,
Sprinkling magic in the air that satisfies our lust!

He will not let me forget the "Venus Bag,"
He knows there will be goodies to tickle his swag!
Our naked emotions are running wild,
He knows the treats will have his head in the clouds!

The "Venus" bag is kept in the truck,
Never know when he needs to fuck!
He could have a stressful day at work,
If he did or didn't, he can get what's under my mini-skirt!

The sex sessions will be heated and intense,
Dazzling him with aromas and suspense!
He likes to be teased and aroused with variety,
The "Venus" got what he desires, it's hot and spicy!

We keep our encounters enticing and fresh,
I keep him amused with pleasurable tests.
He gets a treat every time he makes my juices rain,
Rewarding him keeps him striving to drive me insane!

Craving a Caramel Delight!

Grab my being gently and tightly squeeze me,
As I climb inside of you I am no longer lonely!
I will persist with inspiring your skyscraping ego,
By riding you like a stallion and then drop it low!

As my loving puts your mind on cloud nine,
Kitty grabs your strong pole and make it mine!
The way you work your body makes me shake,
You work it like an out of control rattle snake!

Your brown succulent lips serenades me with a kiss,
Making my booty clap magically supplying endless bliss!
You are clothed in rays of mystery,
Creating miracles as we strive for stability!

Yearning to climb and dance with you like a shiny pole,
Caressing it up and down as I become food for your soul!
You are restored as I parade around in your favorite pumps,
The lingerie I wear creates images of my rump.

Now that your life is filled with fairytales that are exotic,
Your mind is captivated with daydreams without logic!
Your mocha hue hands travels all over my body frame,
Taking my breath away, making my hot nectar rain!

Hey! Mr. Mocha Magic!

Mr. Magic is classy and sexy,
His confidence overshadows his inner complexity!
He will know his queen when he desires to be discovered,
His fondness is inspiring him to secure her before another brother!

Her stilettos will intoxicate him with intense passion,
Lavishing each other with sucking, licking until Juices start Splashing!
It will be like swimming long distance strokes in an Olympic pool,
As their bodies connect, he works her over with his tools!

At last her fantasies activate delights in all the hot spots?
She strives to satisfy his secret need to be on top.
Mr. Magic is wonderful and keeps her dripping with chocolate,
Her skills are sharp and put moves on him with the kitty pocket!

Their connection is enhanced each day with a smile,
As they become recession proof to walk the turbulent miles!
They appreciate exploring each other from the front to the backbone,
Like drinking from a fountain of ecstasy as they loudly groan!

They will keep each other sizzling with needed delight,
Savoring each moment with a twist of ecstasy that's just right!
He is in all honesty a dream come true,
As we wait patiently we ask the question is it him or YOU?

The Techno Love Routine!

Take my photos and make love to me until it refreshes you,
I yearn to hold you because our quality moments together are few!
Now that you have the images, put your hand on your spot and rub it,
Stroke that big cock, while imaging me there, as you sit?!

Standing boldly before you in the sexy lingerie that's red,
You are watching from the web cam fingering myself on the bed!
Looking forward to the time when we are getting our freak on live,
Technology has its place but I'm looking for you to arrive!

Keep working hard on the project that's keeping us apart,
It will be over soon then we will start!
In the meantime, I will keep satisfying you with videos and pictures,
Of my kitty embracing your juicy dick to be soothed with adventures!

Kitty is purring for your warm touch and tongue,
Make it rain with hot juices you are so much fun!
No other man satisfies me like you do Ninja Man,
I can feel the vibration of you inside of me with your hand!

Until we meet again Big Daddy via technology,
Stay focus on the project and know that I miss you greatly!
Instant message me when you need your next fix,
I will respond with a text, email or call to please your dick!

I Desire You Inside Me!

You are so beautiful to me every day,
I crave you every minute in all types of ways!
Your juiciness is stimulating my total being,
Tell me how you love me and know that believing is seeing.

Stand strong because your stature is that of a King,
It's my honor to be crowned as your Queen!
We are wonderful together as one,
You are the leader and I am the helper, what fun!

The way you lick your lips,
Makes me wet all over, do you want to take a sip?
Kiss me from head to toe stop for a moment in the middle,
The way you move your body inside me makes me sizzle!

It's been a long time since we made love,
Yet I only want you and no other man ranks above!
Will you put your other priorities on hold for a moment?
To embrace our passion and get in it!

Until we meet again remain a delight,
Improving your skills daily, you are a stunning sight!
Your image is etched in my soul,
When I see you I am going to grab you and be bold!

My Horny Valentine!

Until we meet again my horny Valentine,
Don't share the dick with anyone, it's mine!
I know what you want and will satisfy you every need,
Riding and licking your cock with ease and pleasing speed!

You love when I stroke your pole with my hot & ready,
Riding you like a jock the flow of my juices is steady.
I get hot just thinking about your big, sweet dick,
Looking forward to you showing my body new tricks!

Keep working your plan and making it happen for us,
Come home soon Big Daddy and let me adore you with lust.
I need our bodies to touch and feel you inside my soul,
Only you can fulfill my love craving and seal this empty hole!

Tears of joy stroll down my cheeks like a water fall,
Because we will be together dancing and having a ball!
As I await your arrival, I have many surprises and treats,
You are so wonderful and deserve the best for being sweet!

Our greatest strength is our ability to feel without a touch,
The stimulation is intense because we miss each other so much.
Our lives seem empty until we are together again,
The time will come when we can dance while drinking gin!

Knock it out the Ballpark and Score!

You spark the flames of my fire and desire,
Sizzling on the inside, I begin to perspire!
Wow! Your presence sets me up for a home run,
Just as I strive to score you touch me and I am done!

It's my turn to knock it out the ballpark,
Yet I'm dazed by your appearance and stiff cock!
Not to be out done, I saddle up to win the race,
Satisfaction guaranteed is the purpose of our pace.

Taking turns to stimulate and delight, you step up to score,
Damn as I ride your pole it makes me want you more and more!
It's always a successful encounter playing on your team,
Each experience is like winning a championship, a fulfilled dream!

When we strive to achieve the same ecstasy goal,
The end results are amazingly nourishing to our soul!
When You and I score, we have a win-win outcome,
Let's keep knocking it out the ballpark connected as one!

We are playing in the major leagues Baby!
There is no time to watch or be lazy.
Be aware of the violation clock, time keeps ticking,
We score with our best skills which includes licking and sticking!

Lipstick on His Dipstick!

Red, pink, bronze, or sparkling lip gloss,
Licking and sucking until I get lock jaws!
The head, shaft and balls my tongue is stroking,
Deep throating the entire dick without choking!

Tick, tock the clock moves minutes to an hour,
As he reaches his peak, his cum gives me a shower!
Oh my! This lipstick gets a surprise,
He is moaning with pleasure I realize!

Caressing and slurping while on my knees,
Saluting the dick with my succulent mouth in order to please!
Juggling the balls in my hands and rubbing the cock on my tongue,
As he watches in amazement he is stunned!

It takes sucking skills to master the dipstick,
It's like a Popsicle on a hot sunny day, lick, and lick!
Embrace his pole with tender, love and care,
Mesmerizing him with my unique style, it's rare!

Nibbling around the head as I stroke up and down the entire length,
I massage it with my mouth and watch the dick gain strength!
Yes, he is satisfied as he trembles with delight,
He said a job well done, your skills are just right!

The Good Ship Lollipop!

Hopping, skipping and jumping,
Tonight we will be humping!
He is geared up and ready to ride,
It is delightful as we glide.

Licking his lollipop, satisfying the taste buds,
This man is built like a sexy stud!
His juices got me salivating,
As I enjoy him all over my body it is elating!

His moans are stirring up my nerves,
I'm getting satisfaction as he is served!
This is how it's done on my ship,
He will always remember this trip!

Bouncing to the saucy caressing beat,
I make sure he stays in heat!
It is my goal to satisfy his every desire,
As I learn what gets him aroused, I am inspired!

Thanks for joining me on this journey,
Look forward to dancing with you at the next party.
Until we meet again my darling friend,
Your disposition helps me to feel like you are a win!

A Powerful Make Out Session!

Ring, Ring he answered the phone,
I want to fuck I said in a sexy tone!
Laughter filled the silence in the air,
He needed time to process the request to be fair!

Come on over baby and ride my pole,
You will get all you need in every hole!
Oh my! It must be my lucky time!
To have a man available to rock my spine!

I got a few tricks to make his knees knock,
As I thrust this pussy on his big cock!
His goal was to stimulate me into ecstasy,
Instead I took him beyond his fantasy!

I vigorously licked and rode him like a pony,
Getty up Daddy, I'm so horny!
Slipping and sliding our bodies moved in unity,
Moaning and groaning he spanked my booty.

Our "making out" sessions are off the chain,
Every episode is unique and wildly insane!
Variety is the spice of life,
We agree to bring our best without strife!

A Joyful Noise Mantra!

Splish, Splash we were taking a bath,
The bumping and grinding made us laugh!
The water and bubbles caused our touch to be slippery,
This is so much fun as we strive for a victory!

Dripping in wetness from our yearning,
As we caress each other his cock is firming!
Oh my, it is getting steamy in this space,
Hot with desires as we gaze face-to-face!

Our bodies are filled with glee,
Can hardly wait to fulfill our fantasy!
Full of surprises to satisfy each other's desire,
As we role play to keep it interesting we are on fire!

The moans are loud and passionate,
We are peaking in sensation and we are resilient!
The mantra is all about chanting with delight,
When the sentiment is mutual our souls become bright!

Sing a joyful noise as you love,
Giving thanks to the One above!
Indulge in the blissful treat,
That you and your lover exchange in heat!

Welcome Spontaneity...Stimulating for Sure!

My get-up-and-go intensifies when I'm with you,
Surprises overflow with teasing moves and lustful clues!
You are my vibrant toy...full of life and pleasure,
No batteries needed to satisfy my cookie treasure!

I hunger for your stiff dick to put me in a trance,
You are my paradise, every time you fuck me it's like a dance!
Wow! My kitty leaps for you automatically when you grab my waist,
You gently rock my booty and satisfy my taste.

We uniformly move to the rhythm of our dance routine,
Your kisses jet me to the moon with sexual rushes like a machine.
Thank you for enhancing my imagination to meet your sexual desire,
The way you roll your hips sets me on fire!

Your manly hugs engulf me like heat from a flame of burning passion,
Your feast is ready, make it do what it do, this pussy is thrashing!
As I squeeze your nipples your excitement notify my hands,
I am traveling and exploring your aroused sexy glands.

How do you want it naked or wrapped in a bow with lace?
Your wish is my command, here to serve you as I sit on your face!
You and I are tied together and nothing else really matter!
The way you stroke, lick and kiss me, has me climbing your ladder.

The Cum Back Kitty!

As the healing takes place after a delicate surgery,
My body is filled with extra sensitive energy!
The dreams of sexual fantasy is enriching my mind,
The brothers keep asking is it time?

The response is no I am unable to share kitty it is still restoring,
Not to be uncaring but their requests, I am ignoring.
I thought my mojo was gone to never come back,
Then kitty started purring to let me know it is on the right track!

Well since the kitty is fresh and renewed,
Who will be the lucky man to be screwed?
It is great to have choices from the past and fresh,
Yet, I have principles to be honored, which one will outlast the rest?

A lot of time and resources have been invested in this cum back kitty,
Only real men need to apply, there is no time for pity!
The kitty is a powerful resource to be shared only with the elite,
Please Baby Please! Quench kitty's desires in and out of the sheets!

Meet me in the middle if you can handle the mission,
Love it unconditional in all types of positions.
It takes a colorful imagination to nourish this prize,
There is assurance that this kitty is sure to hypnotize!

The Molecules Shift in Your Presence!

As I peel away the layers and show my naked soul,
Your manliness is bright and bold!
Could you be my enchanted love?
Or are you a mirage from my deepest desire club?

I am standing with you in your light,
Because together we will shine bright!
You say you are not ready to try again,
Please be encouraged and let's not pretend.

There are no guarantees for us,
We just need to be sure without lust!
Yes, your swag is intoxicating me,
It has me thinking about you as a possibility!

Stay as wonderful as your sweetness projects,
I'm excited about you sharing as you confess!
Tell me how you truly feel,
Be honest as you can about the thrills!

As the color wheel offers variety,
You are my needed King wrapped up in masculinity!
There's no need for us to distrust,
We are each other's keeper, what an adrenaline rush!

Refocusing on the Femininity Within!

Touch me gently with your hands,
So that I will surrender to your commands!
Whisper in my ear how you truly feel,
Yes, We can make this experience real!

Your smell ignites my inner craving
And these desires are amazing!
I'm kissing you on your neck to get a vibe,
That connects us as we unify!

The way you dance so close to me,
Invigorates my secret fantasies!
When you walk up behind me it takes my breath away,
I become thrilled and follow without delay!

As you lead I will do my best to follow,
As we inhale deeply, our fear we swallow!
There are many bench warmers in my face,
Are you going to claim the starter space!

Calling the Booty Bandit!

Hey, "booty bandit" come put out my fire,
I need you kissing me, riding my clit and eating my pussy with desire.
My goodness you are fucking me with that big ass cock,
Your dick stays so hard and keeps my kitty satisfied, I'm in shock.

You have an amazing cock that satisfies on a regular basis.
The things you do for me, keeps my heart singing like a joyful oasis.
I will try as hard as I can to give this hot kitty to you day after day,
You deserve to have the best fucking hear what I say!

Your dick is supposed to get sucked daily, to help support you,
I admire your body; it is solid and sweet as honey dew.
Know that I am here for you and together we all achieve more.
All this fucking has my kitty sore.

I am better today because of the love that you give me,
And I want to say thank you for staying true to our "booty bandit" decree.
Know that you are just one fine man,
Until we meet again keep the dick as hard as you can!

A Blackout Escapade of Pleasure!

Each lovemaking session puts us into a paradise slumber from a round of
amazing sex,
Night after night, we stir the fire in each other for a gratifying climax!
The stimulation keeps the sexual explosion at an all-time high,
It becomes a game for us to see who can please the other with a sigh.

After one of our many escapades, he surprises me with his hard cock,
In my pussy and tickling my clit with a silver bullet vibrator, I am shocked!
As I regain consciousness from a delightful black out,
His boyish smile welcomed me back to reality with high status clout!

I had never experienced such erotic pleasure by my smile!
How could he have known what I needed to feel completely satisfied?
He simply explored my body and listened to my moans,
In order to know what he needed to do to create melodic tones.

The blissfulness of our bodies came alive in each of us,
Our smiles were contagious as we developed another level of trust.
We were so intertwined; as time ticked away we realized we must depart,
this memory will resonate and tickle our hot spots.

Revolutionary Kitty Out-the-Box!

It do, It do, and It did,
The kitty is jumping out as I remove the lid.
Hold up, wait a minute this is a hot box,
It is feisty and ready for a stiff, juicy cock?

The kitty is tight to the touch,
Craving Mr. Big Stuff to cum and satisfy it much!
The grass is kept low, and it responds to a special tickle,
The man that gets it needs a sweet and strong pickle!

This erotic kitten is tender and hot,
It's excited thinking someone is going to hit the spot.
Big Daddy, transform this kitty with your pole,
Penetrate it deeply and blow it like Kenny G on the saxophone with soul!

The revolutionary process will not be televised,
When the kitty squirts its juices, you will be mesmerized!
Amazed by the flexibility of the kitty goddess,
You are thrilled as you reflect and remain modest!

Ain't No Love like My Baby's Love!

Kitty is calling your name,
Take her in your sultry mouth,
she yearns for the vibration from our sex games.
Then work your magic without a doubt.

Make her tremble with cum from your stick,
Taking our freakiness two the next climax,
she loves your big daddy dick
with a lot of sensual & succulent sex!

Kitty is screaming for a refill,
Penetrate her with that juicy miracle,
of your starburst thrills,
The feeling is so deep this gotta be Spiritual!

Baby you are a talented sex artists,
Every encounter is exciting for us,
You keep me growing into a goddess,
My cum temperature is hot enough to bust!

Who's Loving Who?

When loving you is wrong, I am okay with it,
The thought of you erect my tits!
My love is enough but I need your love,
To fly us like peaceful doves.

Your love soothes my pain,
Thank you for keeping me from going insane.
Rock my body with your special swag,
Every episode makes me glad.

The rhythm of your body is a special motion,
Yes, you got the magic potion.
I am mesmerize by the talents you bring,
They have me doing the go-go swing!

Do Wop, Do Wop Chuck Brown sings,
Tonight I'm on top like puppets on strings!
Although I love you with all of my heart,
You have been a fantasy from the start.

Don't Tell the Truth...Don't You Dare!

The lies you speak to me,
Always sound like tweet tweets.
Keep the misinformation to a minimum,
I know the truth, I'm just playing dumb.

You are my fantasy and I love you,
If you tell the truth my heart will be blue.
I would have to let you go,
And I just can't bear loosing you oh no.

Let's create the world we need,
And plant false passionate seeds.
If you dare to be honest at this time,
The truth will be too brutal for my spine.

The truth of who you are will cause too much pain,
Because you belong to another and I am to blame.
I can never replace what I crave,
For you so just dig my grave.

When I Back it Up on You...!

The most amazing position for me was backing my ass up,
As I felt the entire dick in the bottom of my pussy as we fuck.
You were riding me like you were competing for the Triple Crown Derby!
After this session, I just might need a massage and body therapy!

I need to be fucked and made love to.
I need my kitty played with and eaten by you.
I want to suck and ride that big, sweet dick from on top,
I will lick your juicy ass with my tongue until you beg me to stop.

I have been hot and horny for days now and I need to release some tension,
I am going to use the massager to get me a nut and I invite you to listen.
This is just a supplement until you get here,
Please call me from the highway when you are near.

It is my wish that you will receive all this tenderness you hunger,
And as a result get your ass over here and handle me like thunder.
Thank you for answering my horny call,
And now I stand confident and tall!

Nutty Pleasures!

This memory will echo and tickle my sizzling spots.
Your BIG manly dingo DICK keeps this pussy wet and hot!
The after effects keep me singing and dancing,
It seems like the first time every time thanks for the romancing.

Absence does make the heart grow tender because on Saturday night,
Oh! Saturday night was powerful and left a sensation of delight!
We explored new positions that make a lady throw up both hands,
I really like your style and your loving ways drive me wild on demand.

I smile and have to tell kitty to calm down,
Because the mighty dick will be return but had to leave for now.
My pussy just tingles at the thought of having your tongue and fingers,
As well as that precious jewel -THE DICK is the biggest trigger!

Okay, I have to stop now because I want you inside of me,
I look forward to you making sure that I am tucked into bed with glee.
Now that you have fucked me royally and caused nutty pleasures,
These are memories that I will forever treasure!

It's Quickie Time!

Wow! We can do amazing sex tricks,
In a short amount time that's great and quick!
Spontaneity keeps us hot and beaming,
For each other which causes our warmth to start steaming!

The foreplay begins immediately when we connect,
Like a science experiment our bodies get ready for dissect!
We are ravishing each other to get to the satisfactory part,
Time is ticking let the grinding start!

As our bodies heat with passion our breathing become high-speed,
Because we need to explode with ecstasy from this unplanned deed!
Get in there and make it rain with trembling desire,
That has been hidden within and ready to ignite a fire!

This episode is over and the status is we won,
With a spur-of-the-moment encounter that was lots of fun!
A sigh of release fills the air from a fabulous quickie event,
We are thankful for precious time well spent!

I Submit to Your "Billy Club" Fantasy Man!

Let me tell you this fantasy man is blessed with extraordinary tools,
That has me learning like I am back in school!
Awww at last I dream of a man with an enticing "billy club",
To climb on and dance the reggae rub-a-dub!

How will I gulp his entire natural gift with my kitty?
I don't know yet but I will get to the nitty-gritty!
It's been so long since I've witnessed such beauty,
Will he know how to satisfy me and my booty?

No, Dick don't always have to be big to be good,
But don't get it twisted length and width decides the quality of the wood.
When I have the privilege to be blessed with such treasures,
I will allow every inch of my mouth and kitty to define its measure!

As I develop skills to salute his "billy club" in the fantasy land,
It is my belief that the Universal Energy will send this Man!
Imagination you have permission to take over me,
And make this dream a reality!

Learning to Trust the Bondage Activity!

A black satin eye mask is taken out of his bag,
As he puts it over my eyes, he asks do you trust my swag!
My response was I'm not sure about this process as my sight is blocked,
I have never voluntarily surrendered my vision other than to the Holy rock!

Yes, I gave myself permission to trust the man,
That no harm will be caused as I put my life in his hands.
As if being blindfolded wasn't enough then comes hand and feet ties,
What in the world is going on I wonder why…

As these nerves runs rapid from head to toe,
Thoughts of the outcome could be of a friend or foe.
Chants of positive quotes and prayers cried out in my head,
In the event after this pleasurable activity I'm found dead.

The self that doubted, mistrusted, and resisted died that night,
And now I stand before you more confident and with clearer insight!
We started this activity unsure of the closing steps,
He knew I needed to experience this because of what he felt!

If you are asked to participate in a bondage jamboree,
Don't be so quick to judge the end because you are going to be set free!
All things happen for our good,
Even if what we are experiencing is misunderstood!

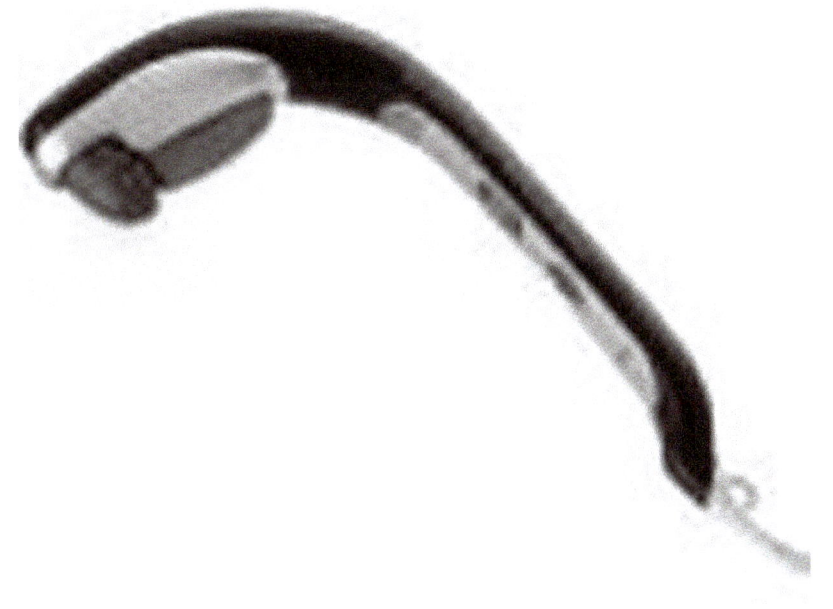

Flirtatious Devices!

Embrace the tiers of your special style,
By branding your partner and driving them wild!
Create a different flavor for 52 weeks,
Wooing with texts, email and even a tweet!

Now be ready to deliver what you speak!
Getting your freak on in and out of the sheets!
Turn on the sensual bouquet within;
arrange each colorful encounter with a grin!

For some, sexual toys can be fun factors,
Stimulating juices to flow like riding a tractor!
Unlock your mind to new ideas of delight,
When it's all said and done-dynamite!

Go ahead and really create magic;
You can add games, sexy lingerie and safe gadgets!
Make sure your mate is responsive and want to play,
Before surprising them as you lay!

Create a warm & cozy space,
To drill and thrill while holding on to their face!
Switch positions and take turns for a win-win,
Gaining momentum as you sit and spin!

Our Instant Connection!

Our eyes meet; our smiles generate an instant connection between us,
Do we act on this emotion or lean back to minimize the rush?
You boldly take a seat near me and speak with a northern accent,
I feel the vibe of excitement as I ponder will this be time well spent?

As we dance to the saxophone playing,
I am going to keep smiling at you as long as you are staying.
Your conversation is piercing my curiosity,
To listen to you although I am captivated by the melody!

What's fascinating me to bond with you?
Are you a deceiver or can I trust that you will be true!
This attraction that I feel has me thinking about the possibility,
Of giving you a chance to know me through discovery!

My fantasy world is including visuals that are risky,
High temperatures, makes your dick ready to salute my pussy!
I want to say go for it Sexy, work your magic on me,
Yes, right there is the spot that drives me wild and sets me free!

The night has turned to morning and we sigh with ecstasy,
As we playfully tease each other and prepare ourselves for reality.
Thank you for a fabulous experience and the beautiful stories,
I appreciate you and hope we continue to stimulate each other's sensory!

Big Daddy CWI by Trade!

Wow! There is so much to your work world,
As I am learning about what you do my head swirls!
You seem to be exposed to many dangerous components,
Some include chemicals, metals, and heavy duty equipment.

Because your days are long and taxing,
With paperwork, inspections, and other duties, home needs to be relaxing!
As soon as you get home from your tedious work,
Your dinner will be ready, a bubble bath too, and yes those special perks!

Where I lack in skills as a Certified Welding Inspector,
I more than make up as your dick protector!
We calibrate our strengths and weaknesses as a united team,
Just thinking about you creates all sorts of day dreams!

Thanks for making the world a better place with your craft,
Creating detailed reports and approving blueprint drafts.
You have enormous responsibilities and an important role,
Come Big Daddy CWI and I will soothe your soul!

During the day you are a Welder by trade,
At night you are "Ninja Man" penetrating my kitty like a blade.
When your dick and my pussy are welded together,
Fire sparks and sensation lingers forever!

Sailing on a Sea of Fantasies!

Love doesn't always strike at the first sight,
Sometimes it starts with lust and then time generates delight!
Pay close attention to specific details,
Before you know it you have the love spell!

Give one another a chance to demonstrate worth,
Spend quality time together for a relationship birth.
Riding the tides of challenges and rewards like a horse,
Holding on tightly and staying the course!

Making fast action, slow and steady,
Tapping into the depths of the sea, we are hot and ready!
Stop! We need to slow it down and to take out time,
Let's not act on the tingle up and down our spine.

Touch me in the morning with your exotic affection,
Relishing each moment lead us in the right direction!
You are the man and that makes you the chief,
Speak with me baby and your expressions can be brief!

You have fascinated my mind with splendid fantasy,
With you in my life, we are pursuing happiness, peace and liberty!
We can face our hang-ups and make them our assets,
We gain positive returns on our efforts, as we track the prospects.

Inconvenient Erotic Healing!

I wasn't ready to let you go yet,
Because we agreed to love and our practice was set.
I didn't need to be holding on to you so tight,
Since you were not available in the beginning but it seemed right.

When we met our chemistry blended very well,
We mesmerized each other with touches, smiles and sensual smells.
I thought I made it clear that I was playing you for your heart,
Why did you run in fear this was clear from the start?

Your timing of leaving is inconveniencing my love for you,
Please distinguish what lies you told from what was true.
We made passionate love under the stars,
It was breathtaking being from Venus and you from Mars!

You told me so many times, you don't play games,
Did you lie or are you trying to drive me insane?
Your unfulfilled promises is hindering my being and sexual healing,
Since you've been gone another man's touch is not appealing.

One thing about life, change is never convenient or calm,
I believed you and didn't hear when you sounded the alarm.
Please forgive me for not paying attention,
To the warning signs that you mention.

Silent Lover!

Turning over every stone looking for my lover,
He was here then he went undercover.
I'm missing him so much,
Every time I think of him, I feel his touch!

Hurry up and come back to me,
I have some new sexy moves just wait and see!
My kitty is popping for your magical works,
Give it to me from the back, then sides, and let me enjoy your perks!

There hasn't been a word from him,
Why doesn't he come see about his gem?
It's been too long since our last duty call,
When we're together we have a ball.

No return calls, texts or email,
What am I supposed to do, I'm losing his smell.
Baby, what is it going to take to see you again?
Yes, we are lover as well as friends!

Silence speaks louder than words sometimes,
Yet your voice is as tantalizing as the rhythm of chimes.
Speak to me honey and let me know your feelings,
Our encounters can be medicine for our healings!

You Touched Me and Now...!

I've been made fragile and whole by your touch,
The sensations have my thoughts out of sync...this is too much!
I pride myself on being in control of me,
How did you get so close for my heart to see?

What do you want from me that you can't get from them?
I'm older, my life is shifting do you see me as a precious gem?
I am a prize for any man, who wants to be dedicated,
And I am not going to be in your rotation to be violated.

So, choose me wisely and no other if you are ready for sure,
Or leave me the hell alone because my love is intense and pure!
Oh my! This glimpse of what we can create seems so real,
I like the way your presence makes me feel!

When I saw your naked body I instantly got moist in my panties,
Damn, your dick is calling me is it the answer to my fantasies?
As I envision the possibilities while rubbing lotion ON your back,
The ripples of your muscles almost caused a heart attack!

I am going to trust life one more time,
Because I know this is for my good as I walk with you in the blind.
As of this moment, you are encouraged to take the lead as a man,
listen closely, act carefully, and take heed to the Master's plan!

It's Just another Fun Day!

A new day is filled with the sun shining brightly,
You are amazing to me and you sweep me off my feet surprisingly!
I have a liking for you that grows daily,
You have my attention and I am hooked on you, Baby.

Wow, you came in the severe snow storm to let me know you care,
My heart is filled with thanks for our affair.
I want to wrap you in my thighs and rock you with my kitty,
And let you fuck me like the first time, bust my cherry.

I never knew my body would respond the way it does for you,
I love the way you make me tremble and do what you do.
Honey, the way you dip in this kitty, cum flows happily,
One nut after another they flow so freely.

Never in my 38 years has love making been so fulfilling,
Sucking your dick, licking your ass, and fucking you are truly thrilling.
I want to make sure that this kitty stays ready for that juicy dick,
And that each encounter is full of surprising tricks.

Mr. Water (H₂O) Bill Man!

Since when did the Kitty become so cheap?
Just A few dollars to perform a phenomenal treat!
This information got to be false,
Or have we become that frightened and lost?

Inflation alone should increase the price;
It seems we've lost sight of what's right?
We need to factor in the huge cost of care,
The maintenance and doctor visits are expensive just to share.

There's a premium to pay to be the boss,
If you want representation without responsibility, then pay the cost.
If love is not your focus and you want pussy for sale,
Then shut up complaining, pay the price or go to hell.

We can only have a mutual business exchange,
When the outcome is win-win, we all have something to gain!
Take a good look at your budget and decide,
Put your money on the table or get somewhere and hide!

The END!

www.ingramcontent.com/pod-product-compliance
Lightning Source LLC
Chambersburg PA
CBHW051214120626
46547CB00013B/1353